WHAT'S INSIDE A
Clock?

ARNOLD RINGSTAD

The Child's World®
childsworld.com

Published by The Child's World®
1980 Lookout Drive • Mankato, MN 56003-1705
800-599-READ • www.childsworld.com

Photographs ©: Rick Orndorf, cover (clock), 1 (clock), 4, 7, 9 (clock back), 9 (dials), 11, 13, 14, 16 (motor), 17, 18, 19, 20 (hammer), 24; Shutterstock Images, cover (gears), 1 (gears), 2, 3 (circuit board), 3 (plug), 5 (glasses), 6 (battery), 6 (gear), 8 (screw), 10, 12, 15, 16 (gear), 20 (gear), 21, 23 (battery), 23 (screw); Praiwun Thungsarn/Shutterstock Images, 3 (screwdriver), 5 (screwdriver), 8 (screwdriver), 22; Shyripa Alexandr/Shutterstock Images, 5 (gloves)

ISBN 9781503832077
LCCN 2018962812

Printed in the United States of America
PA02419

About the Author

Arnold Ringstad lives in Minnesota.

He checks the time on a clock every day.

Contents

Materials and Safety

Materials

- ☐ Clock
- ☐ Phillips screwdriver
- ☐ Safety glasses
- ☐ Work gloves

Safety

- Always be careful with sharp objects, such as screwdrivers.

- Remove the battery before taking the clock apart.

- Wear work gloves to protect your hands from sharp edges.

- Wear safety glasses in case pieces snap off.

Clock

Phillips screwdriver

work gloves

Safety glasses

Inside a Clock

People use clocks every day. These machines keep track of time. They help people think about when things will happen. Some clocks have screens. Others have moving hands. Clocks with alarms can even help people wake up. How does a clock work? What's inside?

Alarm bells

Battery compartment

Alarm motor

Alarm hammer

Quartz movement

Back

Hands

Opening the Clock

Screws hold the back of the clock together. Unscrew them to remove the back. The back contains the battery. It has a switch to turn the alarm on or off. It also has two **dials**. One dial lets people set the time. Another dial lets people set when the alarm will sound.

Safety Note
Be careful when removing the screws.

Inside of
the back

Dials

Inside the Case

The inside of the clock is mostly empty. There is a small black box near the center. This is the part that actually keeps time. It is called a **quartz** movement. Wires carry electricity from the battery into the black box. The dials on the clock's back also connect to the box.

The Vibrating Crystal

The quartz movement has many parts inside. There is a **circuit board**. The circuit board gets electricity from the battery. The circuit board has a quartz crystal on it. The crystal is in a small silver tube. The circuit board makes the quartz crystal **vibrate** very fast.

Safety Note

The quartz movement might have sharp
parts inside, so be careful when handling it.

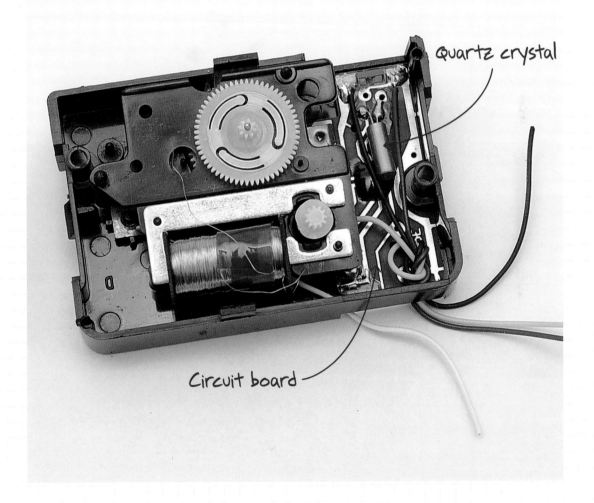

Quartz crystal

Circuit board

Telling Time

The quartz crystal vibrates thousands of times per second. It always vibrates at the same speed.

The circuit board tracks these vibrations. It knows how many vibrations make up one second. It creates an electrical signal each second.

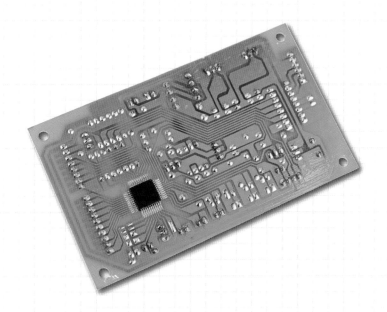

Motor and Gears

The circuit board sends its signals to a tiny motor. The motor turns a set of **gears**. These gears turn the hands of the clock.

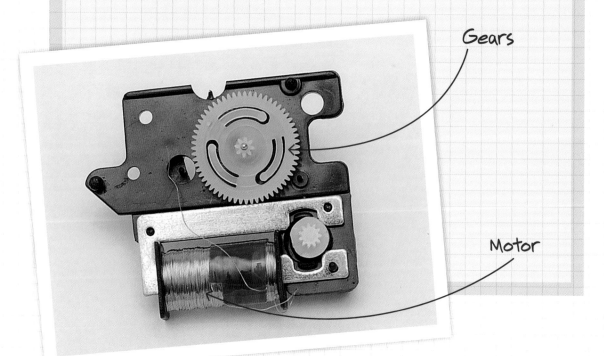

Gears

Motor

The turning gears move the hands of the clock.

Waking Up

This clock has an alarm in it. There is a motor inside the case. The motor is attached to a small hammer. When the motor gets a signal from the quartz movement, it moves the hammer back and forth. The hammer strikes the bells. This makes a loud ringing noise. Time to wake up!

Bells

Motor

Hammer

Reusing a Clock

We've taken apart a clock and learned what's inside. Now what? Here are some ideas for how to reuse the parts of a clock. Can you think of any more?

- **A New Clock:** If the quartz movement still works, take it out of the case and see if you can get it to work without the case. Can you put it into a new case?

- **Make an Instrument:** Remove the alarm bells. Strike them with different objects, such as a pencil or your finger. Can you change the sound they make?

Glossary

circuit board (SUR-kit BORD): A circuit board is a piece of material that holds computer chips, switches, and other parts. Inside the quartz movement, a circuit board holds the quartz crystal and helps tell time.

dials (DYE-uhlz): Dials are things that a person spins in order to use an object. On the back of the clock, users can turn dials to set the time and the alarm.

gears (GEERZ): Gears are toothed wheels that turn together when they rotate. Inside the clock, gears transfer motion from the motor to the hands.

quartz (KWORTS): Quartz is a type of hard mineral. Quartz vibrates at a particular rate, which makes it useful for building clocks.

vibrate (VYE-brate): When you make something vibrate, it shakes back and forth quickly. Inside the quartz clock, a quartz crystal vibrates.

To Learn More

IN THE LIBRARY

Holzweiss, Kristina. *Amazing Makerspace DIY with Electricity*. New York, NY: Scholastic, 2018.

Nagelhout, Ryan. *The Problem with Early Clocks: Oops!* New York, NY: Gareth Stevens Publishing, 2016.

Vogel, Julia. *Measuring Time: The Clock*. Mankato, MN: The Child's World, 2013.

ON THE WEB

Visit our website for links about taking apart a clock: **childsworld.com/links**

Note to Parents, Teachers, and Librarians: We routinely verify our Web links to make sure they are safe and active sites. So encourage your readers to check them out!

Index